Happy Birthday
Love Tyler & Jordie

NATURE WATCH
CROCODILES

Barbara Taylor

Consultant: Dr. Richard Griffiths,
Durrell Institute of Conservation and Ecology

LORENZ BOOKS

C O N

First published in 2000 by Lorenz Books

© 2000 Anness Publishing Limited

Lorenz Books is an imprint of Anness Publishing Limited
Hermes House, 88–89 Blackfriars Road, London SE1 8HA

Published in the USA by Lorenz Books, Anness Publishing Inc.,
27 West 20th Street, New York, NY 10011;
(800) 354–9657.

This edition distributed in Canada by Raincoast Books, 8680
Cambie Street, Vancouver, British Columbia, V6P 6M9.

A CIP catalogue record for this book is
available from the British Library

ISBN 1-85967-640-5

Publisher: Joanna Lorenz
Managing Editor, Children's Books: Gilly Cameron Cooper
Senior Editor: Nicole Pearson
Editors: Peter Harrison; Charlotte Hurdman
Designer: Ann Samuel, Rita Wuthrich
Picture Researcher: Wendy Wilders
Illustrators: Linden Artists
Production Controller: Yolande Denny
Editorial Reader: Jonathan Marshall

Printed and bound in Singapore

10 9 8 7 6 5 4 3 2 1

PICTURE CREDITS
b=bottom, t=top, c= center, l= left, r= right
ABPL: 35t/C Haagner, 5c,22b/C Hughes, 28b/M Harvey,
5tl,18bl/R de la Harper, 36b,37t/S Adev, 23b; Ancient Art &
Architecture Collection, 42br; BBC Natural History Unit: /A
Shah, 25t/J Rotman, 10bl/M Barton, 8bl/P Oxford, 49br/T
Pooley, 35c; Biofotos: /B Rogers, 43t; Bruce Coleman: /Animal
Ark, 3tr,47tl/CB&DW Frith, 55br/E&P Bauer, 56b/G Cozzi,
38b/J McDonald, 47c/LC Marigo, 39bl,41br,46t,49c/M Plage,
52c/R Williams, 6br,63t; CM Dixon: 8br; e.t. archive: 26bl; FLPA:
/G Lacz, 31tl/W Wisniewski, 16b,64t; G Webb: 17c,57b, Heather
Angel: 19cr,60b; M&P Fogden: 14t,21bl,28t,46c,33cl,47b,58t,62t;
Mary Evans Picture Library: 4bl,20br,41bl; Natural History
Museum, London: 50b,51c; Nature Photographers Ltd/EA James,
10br/R Tidman, 9b/SC Bisserot, 26br; NHPA: 38t,52t/D
Heuchlin, 11c,23t,34t,37c,45(both),58b,59tr,59b,61tl/E Soder,
55bl/H&V Ingen, 7bl/J Shaw, 49t/K Schafer, 27t/M Harvey,
20bl/M Wendler, 3br,5tr,41c,57cr,61tr,61b/N Wu, 27b/NJ
Dennis, 39cl,61c/O Rogge, 16tl/P Scott, 58c/S Robinson, 15br; :
Oxford Scientific Films/A Bee, 55tr/B Wright, 11tr/Breck P
Kent, 59tl/E Robinson, 4tr,30b/ER Degginger, 7cr/F
Ehrenstrom, 6tr/F Schneidermeyer, 15cl/F Whitehead, 40t/J
Macdonald, 9c/J McCammon, 56t /J Robinson, 20tl/K
Westerkov, 52b/M Deeble&V Stone,
17tl,19cl,22tl,29t,29b,33b,36t,39cr/M Fogden, 15tl/M Pitts,
48b,endpapers/M Sewell, 8t/O Newman, 41t/R Davies, 43b/S
Leszczynski, 15cr,53b,57t/S Osolinski, 6bl,12tr,30t,31cl,62b,43c/S
Turner, 49bl/W Shattil, 21t; Planet Earth: /A&M Shah, 25c/B
Kenney, 34b/C Farnetti, 32b/D Kjaer, 39tl/D Maitland,
40b/DA Ponton, 19b/G Bell, 23c/J Lythgoe, 32t/J Scott,
17tr,24bl,25b,31bl/JA Provenza, 18tr/K Lucas,
1,2tl,4–5,11bl,44t,53tl(both),57cl,64b/M&C
Denis-Huot, 14cl/N Greaves, 24tl/P
Stephenson, 60t /R de la Harper,
33tl,42t,46b; Survival Anglia: /F
Koster, 44b,2bl/M Linley, 54t/M
Price, 42bl/V Sinha, 9t,35cr;
Twentieth Century Fox: 54b

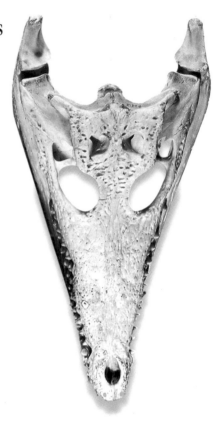

TENTS

What is a Crocodilian?

Crocodilians are scaly, armor-clad reptiles that include crocodiles, alligators, caimans and gharials. They are survivors from a prehistoric age—their relatives first lived on the earth with the dinosaurs nearly 200 million years ago. Today, they are the dinosaurs' closest living relatives, apart from birds.

Crocodilians are fierce predators. They lurk motionless in rivers, lakes and swamps, waiting to snap up prey with their enormous jaws and strong teeth. Their prey ranges from insects, frogs and fish to birds and large mammals, such as deer and zebras. Very few crocodilians regularly attack and kill humans. Most are timid. Crocodilians usually live in warm, tropical places in or near freshwater, and some live in the sea. They hunt and feed mainly in the water, but crawl onto dry land to sunbathe, build nests and lay their eggs.

▲ SCALY TAILS
Like many crocodilians, an American alligator uses its long, strong tail to swim through the water. The tail moves from side to side to push the alligator along. The tail is the same length as the rest of the body.

Long, strong tail has flat sides to push aside water for swimming.

► CROCODILIAN CHARACTERISTICS
With its thick, scaly skin, huge jaws and powerful tail, this American alligator looks like a living dinosaur. Its eyes and nostrils are on top of its head so that it can see and breathe when the rest of its body is underwater. On land, crocodilians slither along on their bellies, but they can lift themselves up on their four short legs to walk.

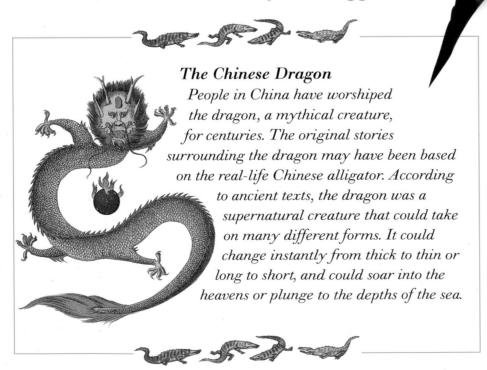

The Chinese Dragon
People in China have worshiped the dragon, a mythical creature, for centuries. The original stories surrounding the dragon may have been based on the real-life Chinese alligator. According to ancient texts, the dragon was a supernatural creature that could take on many different forms. It could change instantly from thick to thin or long to short, and could soar into the heavens or plunge to the depths of the sea.

▲ TALKING HEADS

Huge, powerful jaws lined with sharp teeth make Nile crocodiles killing machines. They are some of the world's largest and most dangerous reptiles. The teeth are used to attack and grip prey, but are useless for chewing. Prey has to be swallowed whole or in chunks.

► SHUTEYE

Although this spectacled caiman has its eyes shut, it is probably not asleep, but dozing. Two butterflies are basking in safety on the caiman's head. Predators will not dare attack it because the caiman is still sensitive to what is going on around it, even though its eyes are shut.

► SOAKING UP THE SUN

Nile crocodiles sun themselves on a sandbank. This is called basking and warms the body. Crocodilians are cold-blooded, which means that their body temperature is affected by their surroundings. They have no fur or feathers to keep them warm, nor can they shiver to warm up. They move in and out of the water to warm up or cool down.

The scales on the back are usually much more bony than those on the belly.

Scaly skin covers the whole body for protection and camouflage.

Did you know? Most crocodilians live for about 50 years but some live up to 100.

Eyes and nostrils on top of the head

The digits (toes) of each foot are slightly webbed.

American alligator (*Alligator mississippiensis*)

Long snout with sharp teeth to catch prey

Croc or Gator?

There are 13 species (kinds) of crocodile, two species of alligator, six species of caiman and two species of gharial. Gharials have distinctive long, slender snouts, but crocodiles and alligators are often more difficult to tell apart. Crocodiles usually have longer, more pointed snouts than alligators. Crocodiles also have one very large tooth sticking up from each side of the bottom jaw when they close their mouths.

▲ CAIMAN EYES
Most caimans have bonier ridges between their eyes than alligators. These ridges help strengthen the skull and look like glasses people wear to help them see. Caimans are usually smaller than alligators.

KEY
- crocodiles
- alligators/caimans
- gharials

▲ WHERE IN THE WORLD?
Crocodiles are the most widespread crocodilian and live in Central and South America, Africa, southern Asia and Australia. Caimans live in Central and South America, while alligators live in the southeastern United States and China. The gharial is found in southern Asia, while the false gharial lives in Southeast Asia.

▼ A CROCODILE'S SMILE
With its mouth closed, a crocodile's fourth tooth in the lower jaw fits into a notch on the outside of the upper jaw. No teeth can be seen on the bottom jaw of an alligator's closed mouth.

Chinese alligator
(*Alligator sinensis*)

▲ COOL ALLIGATOR
There are two species of alligator, the Chinese alligator (*shown above*) and the American alligator. Alligators are the only crocodilians that can survive cooler temperatures and live outside the tropics.

▶ DIFFERENT SNOUTS

Crocodilian snouts are different shapes and sizes because of the food they eat and the way they live. Gharials and crocodiles have narrow, pointy snouts suited to eating fish. Alligators, and caimans have wider, rounder snouts that can manage larger prey, such as birds and mammals. Their jaws are strong enough to overpower victims that are even larger than they are.

Gharial

Caiman

Crocodile

◀ OUT TO SEA

The enormous saltwater crocodile, often called the saltie, has the largest range of all the crocodilians. It is found from the east coast of India through Southeast Asia to the Philippines, New Guinea and northern Australia. Saltwater crocodiles are one of the few species found far out to sea, but they do live in freshwater rivers and lakes as well.

▶ POT NOSE

Two species of gharial, the gharial, or gavial, and the false gharial, live in the rivers, lakes and swamps of southern Asia. The name comes from the bump on the nose of the male gharial, which is called a ghara (pot) in the Hindi language. Some experts say the false gharial is a species of crocodile and is therefore not really part of the gharial family.

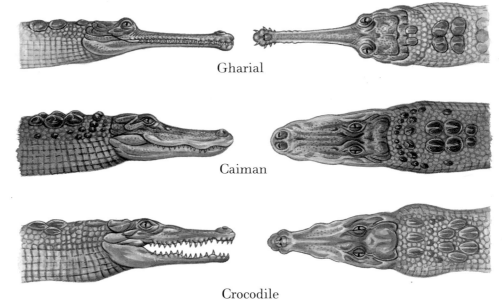

Adult male gharials have a conspicuous bump at the tip of their snouts.

Gharial
(*Gavialis gangeticus*)

Large and Small

Can you imagine a crocodile that weighs as much as three cars? A big, 23-foot-long saltwater crocodile is as heavy as this. It is the heaviest living reptile in the world. Other enormous crocodilians include Nile crocodiles, gharials and American alligators, which can reach lengths of 18 feet or more. Very large crocodiles and alligators are now rare because many are hunted and killed for their meat and skins before they grow to their maximum size. The smallest species of crocodilian are the dwarf caimans of South America and the African dwarf crocodile. These forest-dwelling reptiles grow to about 5 feet long.

▲ **BIGGEST CAIMAN**
The black caiman is the largest of the caimans. It can grow to over 19 ft long and is the biggest predator in South America. Black caimans live in the flooded Amazon forest, around lakes and slow-flowing rivers. They hunt at night for capybara, turtles, deer and fish.

▲ **A CROC IN EACH HAND**
A person holds a baby Orinoco crocodile (*top*) and a baby spectacled caiman (*bottom*). As adults, the Orinoco crocodile will be twice the length of the caiman, reaching about 16 ft. You can clearly see how the crocodile has a longer, thinner snout than the caiman.

Crocodile God
The ancient Egyptians worshiped the crocodile-headed god Sebek. He was the god of lakes and rivers, and is shown here with Pharaoh Amenhotep III. A shrine to Sebek was built at Shedet. Here, a Nile crocodile decorated with gold rings and bracelets lived in a special pool. It was believed to be the living god. Other crocodiles were also treated with great respect and hand-fed on meat, cakes, milk and honey.

◄ **SUPER-SNOUTED CROCODILE**

The mugger crocodile of India and surrounding lands has the broadest snout of all crocodiles, making it look more like an alligator. Adult males reach about 13 ft long. The name mugger comes from its habit of snatching fish out of people's fishing nets.

◄ **SMALLEST CROCODILIAN**

Cuvier's dwarf caiman is about a fifth of the size of a giant saltwater crocodile, yet it would still only just fit on your bed! It lives in the rainforests of the Amazon basin in South America. It has particularly tough, armored skin to protect it from rocks in fast-flowing rivers. It has a short snout and high, smooth skull. Its short snout does not prevent it from eating a lot of fish.

Did you know? Male alligators keep growing until they are 15 years old.

► **MONSTER CROC**

The huge Nile crocodile is the biggest and strongest freshwater predator in Africa. It can grow up to 19 ft long and eats any prey it can overpower, including monkeys, antelopes, zebras and sometimes, people. Nile crocodiles probably kill at least 300 people a year in Africa. Despite its name, the Nile crocodile is not just found along the Nile but also lives in rivers, lakes and swamps through most of tropical Africa.

Scaly Skin

The outside of a crocodilian's body is completely covered in a suit of leathery armor. It is made up of rows of tough scales, called scutes, that are set into a thick layer of skin. Some scutes have small bony disks inside them. Most crocodilians have bony scutes only on their backs, but some, such as caimans, have them on their bellies as well. The tail never contains bony scutes, but it does have thicker tail scutes. As crocodilians grow, bigger scutes develop under the old ones. Crocodilians do not get rid of their old scaly skin in a big piece, like a snake, or in patches like a lizard. Old scutes drop off one at a time, just as humans lose flakes of skin all the time. On the head, the skin is fused directly to the bones of the skull without any muscles or fat in between.

Tricky Alligator

A Guyanese myth tells how the Sun was tricked by an alligator into letting him guard his fishponds from a thief. The thief was the alligator, and to punish him the Sun slashed his body, forming the scales. The alligator promised the Sun his daughter for a wife. He had no children, so he carved her from a tree. The Sun and the woman's offspring were the Carob people.

▲ COLOR CHANGE

Most crocodilians are brightly colored or patterned as babies, but these features usually fade as they grow older. They have more or less disappeared in fully-grown adults. The colors and patterns may help with camouflage by breaking up the outline of the body.

▲ NECK ARMOR

Heavy, bony scutes pack tightly together to create a rigid and formidable armor on the back and neck of an African dwarf crocodile. Even the scutes on the sides of its body and tail are heavily armored. This species lives in the dwindling rainforests of West and Central Africa. The small size and bony armor of the dwarf crocodile has saved it so far from being hunted for its skin.

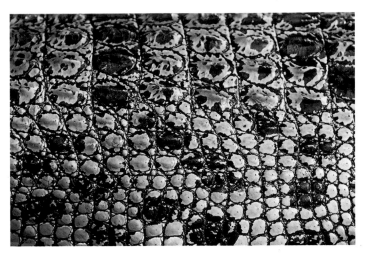

▲ MISSING SCALES

The gharial has fewer rows of armored scutes along its back than other crocodilians. Adults have four rows of deeply ridged back scutes, whereas other crocodilians have two or four extra rows in the middle of the back. The scutes on the sides and belly are unarmored.

▲ BONY BACK

The belly of a saltwater crocodile does not have bony plates in the scutes. You can see the difference in this close-up. Large, bony back scutes are shown at the top of the picture, and the smaller, smoother belly scutes are at the bottom. The scutes are arranged in rows.

► EXTRA ARMOR

This close-up shows the skin of a dwarf caiman—the most heavily armored crocodilian. It has strong bones in the scutes on its belly as well as its back. This provides protection from predators. Even its eyelids are protected by bony plates.

Did you know? The scales of the black caiman are as tough as the heel of a boot.

► ALBINO ALLIGATOR

An albino crocodilian would not survive long in the wild. It does not blend in well with its surroundings, making it easy prey. Those born in captivity in zoos or crocodile farms may survive to adulthood. True albinos are white with pink eyes. White crocodilians with blue eyes are not true albinos.

American alligator
(*Alligator mississippiensis*)

Bodies and Bones

The crocodilian body has changed very little over the last 200 million years. It is superbly adapted to life in the water. Crocodilians can breathe with just their nostrils above the surface. Underwater, ears and nostrils close, and a transparent third eyelid sweeps across the eye for protection. Crocodilians are the only reptiles with ear flaps. Inside the long, lizard-like body a bony skeleton supports and protects the lungs, heart, stomach and other soft organs. The stomach is in two parts, one for grinding food, the other for absorbing (taking in) nutrients. Unlike other reptiles, which have a single-chambered heart, a crocodilian's heart has four chambers, like a mammal's. This allows the heart to pump more oxygen-rich blood to the brain during a dive. The thinking part of its brain is more developed than in other reptiles. This enables a crocodilian to learn things rather than act only on instinct.

▲ **THROAT FLAP**
A crocodilian has no lips, so it is unable to seal its mouth underwater. Instead, two special flaps at the back of the throat keep water from filling the mouth and flowing into the lungs. This enables the crocodile to open its mouth underwater to catch and eat prey without drowning.

Did you know? A saltwater crocodile can stay underwater for more than an hour.

◄ **PREHISTORIC LOOKS**
These American alligators look much like their crocodilian ancestors that lived with the dinosaurs long ago. Crocodilians are the largest living reptiles. The heaviest is the saltwater crocodile which can reach up to 2,420 lbs.

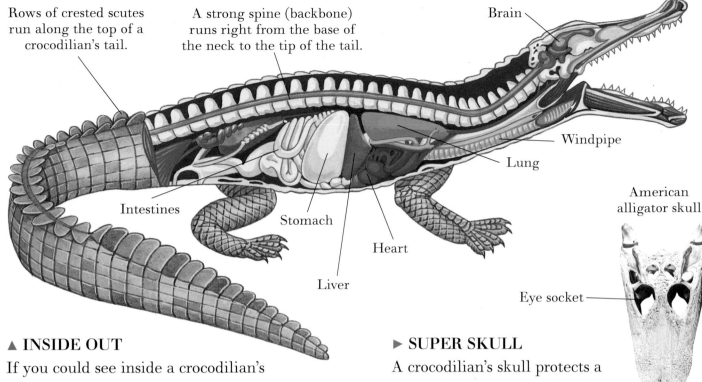

Rows of crested scutes run along the top of a crocodilian's tail.

A strong spine (backbone) runs right from the base of the neck to the tip of the tail.

Brain

Windpipe

Lung

Intestines

Stomach

Heart

Liver

American alligator skull

Eye socket

American crocodile skull

▲ INSIDE OUT

If you could see inside a crocodilian's body you would see a mixture of reptile, bird and mammal features. The crocodilian's brain and shoulder blades are like a bird's. Its heart, diaphragm and efficient breathing system are similar to those of mammals. The stomach and digestive system are those of a reptile, as they deal with food that cannot be chewed.

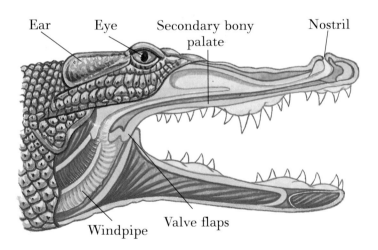

Ear   Eye   Secondary bony palate   Nostril

Windpipe   Valve flaps

▲ WELL-DESIGNED

A view inside the head of a crocodilian shows the ear, eye and nostril openings set high up in the skull. The bones in the mouth are joined together to create a secondary bony palate that separates the nostrils from the mouth. Flaps of skin form a valve, sealing off the windpipe underwater.

▶ SUPER SKULL

A crocodilian's skull protects a brain that is more developed than any other reptile's. The skull is wider and more rounded in alligators (*top*), and long and triangular in crocodiles (*bottom*). Behind the eye sockets are two large holes where jaw muscles attach to the skull.

▶ STOMACH STONES

Crocodilians swallow objects, such as pebbles, to help break down their food. These gastroliths (stomach stones) churn around inside part of the stomach, helping to cut up food so it can be digested. Some very unusual gastroliths have been found, such as bottles, coins, a whistle and a thermos.

13

Jaws and Teeth

The mighty jaws of a crocodilian and its impressive rows of spiky teeth are lethal weapons for catching prey. Crocodilians have two or three times as many teeth as a human. The sharp, jagged teeth at the front of the mouth, called canines, are used to pierce and grip prey. The force of the jaws closing drives these teeth, like a row of knives, deep into a victim's flesh. The short, blunt molar teeth at the back of the mouth are used for crushing prey. Crocodilian teeth are useless for chewing food, and the jaws cannot be moved sideways to chew either. Food has to be swallowed whole, or torn into chunks. The teeth are constantly growing. If a tooth falls out, a new one grows through to replace it.

▲ **MEGA JAWS**
The jaws of a Nile crocodile close with tremendous force. They sink into their prey with tons of crushing pressure. Yet the muscles that open the jaws are weak. A thick rubber band over the snout can easily hold a crocodile's jaws shut.

◄ **NEW TEETH FOR OLD**
Each tooth is set in a socket and held in place by connective tissue. Throughout a crocodilian's life, the old teeth fall out and new teeth underneath take their place. Teeth last up to two years before falling out. Alternate teeth are replaced together, so that not all the teeth in one part of the mouth are lost at the same time.

◀ **LOTS OF TEETH**

The gharial has more teeth than any other crocodilian, around 110. Its teeth are also smaller than those of other crocodilians and are all the same size. The narrow, beak-like snout and long, thin teeth of the gharial are geared to grabbing fish with a sweeping sideways movement of the head. The sharp teeth interlock to trap and impale the slippery prey.

CHARMING

Crocodilian teeth are sometimes made into necklaces. People wear them as decoration or lucky charms. In South America, the Montana people of Peru believe they will be protected from poisoning by wearing a crocodile tooth.

▲ **BABY TEETH**

A baby American alligator is born with a full set of 80 teeth when it hatches from its egg. Baby teeth are not as sharp as adult teeth and are more fragile. They are like tiny needles. In young crocodiles, the teeth at the back of the mouth usually fall out first. In adults, it is the teeth at the front that are replaced more often.

Did you know? A Nile crocodile may use 45 sets of teeth by the time it is 12 ft long.

▶ **GRABBING TEETH**

A Nile crocodile grasps a lump of prey ready for swallowing. If prey is too large to swallow whole, the crocodile grips the food firmly in its teeth and shakes its head hard so that any unwanted pieces are shaken off.

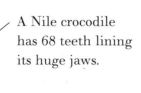

A Nile crocodile has 68 teeth lining its huge jaws.

On the Move

Have you ever seen a film of an alligator gliding through the water with slow, S-shaped sweeps of its powerful tail? Crocodilians move gracefully and easily in the water, using very little energy and keeping most of their body hidden under the surface. Legs lie close alongside bodies to make them streamlined, and cut down drag from the water. They may be used as rudders to change course. On land, the short legs of crocodilians make their walk look slow and clumsy, but they can move quite fast if they need to. Some can gallop at 11 miles per hour when running for short distances of up to 295 feet. Crocodilians also move by means of the belly slide. With side-to-side twists of the body, the animal uses its legs to push along on its belly. This tobogganing movement is useful for fast escapes but is also used to slip quietly into the water.

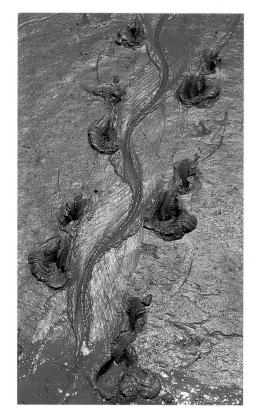

▲ **BEST FOOT FORWARD**
The tracks of a saltwater crocodile in the mud show how its legs move in sequence. The right front leg goes forward first, then the back left leg. The front left leg goes forward next, and finally the right back leg moves. If the legs on the same side moved one after the other, the crocodile would overbalance.

▼ **THE HIGH WALK**
To move on land, crocodilians hold their legs underneath the body, lifting most of the tail off the ground. This is called the high walk. It is very different from the walk of a lizard, which keeps its legs sprawled out at the sides of its body. The tail is dragged behind the body in the high walk, but if the animal starts to run, the tail swings from side to side. A special ankle joint lets crocodilians twist and turn their legs in the high walk.

▲ FLOATING AROUND

This Nile crocodile is floating near the surface of Lake Tanganyika, Tanzania, Africa. It is holding its feet out to the sides for balance. The toes and the webbing between them are spread out for extra stability. In the water, the crocodile floats with its tail down, but as it moves its body becomes horizontal.

► TAIL WALKING

Some crocodilians can leap straight up out of the water. They seem to be walking on their tails in the same way that a dolphin can travel backward on its strong tail. This movement is, however, unusual. Large crocodiles will also spring upward, propelled by their back legs, to grab prey unawares.

► FEET AND TOES

On the front feet, crocodilians have five separate digits (toes). These sometimes have webbing (skin) stretched between them. The back feet are always webbed to help them balance and move in the water. There are only four toes on the back feet. The fifth toe is just a small bone inside the foot.

▲ THE GALLOP

The fastest way for a crocodilian to move on land is to gallop. Only a few crocodiles, such as the Johnston's crocodile shown above, make a habit of moving like this. In a gallop, the back legs push the crocodilian forward in a leap, and the front legs stretch out to catch the body as it lands at the end of the leap. Then the back legs swing forward to push the animal forward again.

Temperature Check

Soon after the sun rises, the first alligators heave themselves out of the river and flop down on the bank. The banks fill up quickly as more alligators join the first, warming their scaly bodies in the sun's rays. As the hours go by and the day becomes hotter, the alligators open their toothy jaws wide to cool down. Later in the day, they may go for a swim or crawl into the shade to cool off. As the air chills at night, the alligators slip back into the water again. This is because water stays warmer for longer at night than the land.

Crocodilians are cold-blooded, which means their body temperature varies with outside temperatures. To warm up or cool down, they move to warm or cool places. Their ideal body temperature is between 85 and 95°F.

▲ MUD PACK
A spectacled caiman is buried deep in the mud to keep cool during the hot, dry season. Mud is like water and does not get as hot or as cold as dry land. It also helps to keep the caiman's scaly skin free from parasites and biting insects.

◄ SOLAR PANELS
The crested scutes on the tail of a crocodilian are like the bony plates on armored dinosaurs. They act like solar panels, picking up heat when the animal basks in the sun. They also open to let as much heat as possible escape from the body to cool down the body.

◄ UNDER THE ICE

An alligator can survive under a layer of ice as long as it keeps a breathing hole open. Only alligators stay active at temperatures as low as 53 or 59°F. They do not eat, however, because the temperature is too low for their digestive systems to work.

▼ OPEN WIDE

While a Nile crocodile suns itself on a rock it also opens its mouth in a wide gape. Gaping helps to prevent the crocodile from becoming too hot. The breeze flowing over the wide, wet surfaces of the mouth and tongue dries the moisture and, in turn, cools the blood. If you lick your finger and blow on it softly, you will notice that it feels a lot cooler.

▲ ALLIGATOR DAYS

Alligators follow a distinct daily routine when the weather is good, moving in and out of the water at regular intervals. They also enter the water if they are disturbed. In winter, alligators retreat into dens and become sleepy because their blood cools and slows them down.

► MEAL BREAKS

Being cold-blooded is quite useful in some ways. These alligators can bask in the sun without having to eat very much or very often. Warm-blooded animals such as mammals have to eat regularly. They need to eat about five times as much food as reptiles to keep their bodies warm.

Crocodilian Senses

The senses of sight, sound, smell, taste and touch are much more powerful in a crocodilian than in other living reptiles. They have good eyesight and can see in color. Their eyes are also adapted to seeing well in the dark, which is useful because they hunt mainly at night. Crocodilians also have acute hearing. They sense the sounds of danger or prey moving nearby and listen for the barks, coughs and roars of their own species at mating time. Crocodilians also have sensitive scales along the sides of their jaws, which help them to feel and capture prey.

▲ **NOISY GATOR**
An American alligator bellows loudly during courtship. Noises such as hissing or snarling, are made at enemies. Young alligators call for help from adults. Small ear slits behind the eyes are kept open when the animal is out of the water. Flaps close to protect the ears when the animal submerges.

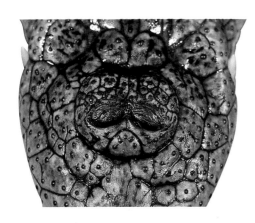

Did you know? Crocodiles shake their ear flaps up and down when they are angry.

▲ **SMELL DETECTORS**
A Nile crocodile picks up chemical signals through the nostrils at the tip of its snout. These messages help it detect prey and others of its kind. Crocodiles can smell food over long distances. They are known to have come from as far away as 2 mi. to feed together on the carcass of a large animal.

Crocodile Tears
According to legend, crocodiles cry to make people feel so sorry for them that they come near enough for the crocodiles to catch them. Crocodiles are also supposed to shed tears of remorse before finishing a meal. It is said that people cry crocodile tears when they seem to be sorry for something but really are not. Real-life crocodiles cannot cry but sometimes look as if they are.

► TASTY TONGUE

Inside the gaping mouth of an American crocodile is a wide, fleshy tongue. It is joined to the bottom of the mouth and does not move, so it plays no part in catching prey. We know that crocodilians have taste buds lining their mouths because some prefer one type of food to another. They can tell the difference between sweet and sour tastes. They also have salt glands on their tongues that get rid of excess salt. Salt builds up in the body over time if the animal lives in the sea or a very dry environment.

◄ GLOW-IN-THE-DARK EYES

A flashlight shone into a crocodile farm at night makes the dark glow eerily with a thousand living lights. The scientific explanation is that a special layer at the back of the eye reflects light back into the front of the eye. This ensures that the eye catches as much light as possible. Above water, crocodilians see well and are able to spot prey up to 295 ft away. Underwater, an inner, transparent lid covers the eye, making vision foggy, like looking through thick goggles.

► A PREDATOR'S EYE

The eye of a spectacled caiman, like all crocodilians, has both upper and lower lids. A third eyelid at the side, called a nictating (blinking) membrane, moves across to clean the eye's surface. The dark, vertical pupil narrows to a slit to stop bright light from damaging the eye. At night, the pupil opens wide to let any available light into the eye. A round pupil, such as a human's, cannot open as wide.

Food and Hunting

How would it feel to wait up to two years for a meal? Amazingly, a big crocodile can probably survive this long between meals. It lives off fat stored in its tail and other parts of its body. Crocodilians eat a lot of fish, but their strong jaws will snap up anything that wanders too close, from birds, snakes and turtles to raccoons, zebras, cattle and horses. They also eat dead animals. Young crocodilians eat small animals such as insects, snails and frogs.

Most crocodilians sit and wait for their food to come to them, which saves energy. They also catch their meals by stalking and surprising prey. The three main ways of capturing and killing food are lunging toward prey, leaping up out of the water and sweeping their jaws open from side to side through the water. Most crocodilians hunt at night. They eat every part of their prey, including the bones.

▲ SURPRISE ATTACK
A Nile crocodile lunges from the water at an incredible speed to grab a wildebeest in its powerful jaws. It is difficult for the wildebeest to jump back, as the river bank slopes steeply into the water. The crocodile will plunge back into the water, dragging its prey with it in order to drown it.

▼ BOLD BIRDS
Large crocodiles feed on big wading birds such as this saddlebill stork. Birds, however, often seem to know when they are in no danger from a crocodile. Plovers have been seen standing on the gums of crocodiles and even pecking at their teeth for leftovers. A marabou stork was once seen stealing a fish right out of a crocodile's mouth.

▶ SMALLER PREY

A dwarf caiman lies in wait to snap up a tasty bullfrog. Small species of crocodilian like this caiman, as well as young crocodilians, eat a lot of frogs and toads. Youngsters also snap up beetles, spiders, giant water bugs and small fishes. They will leap into the air to catch dragonflies and other insects hovering over the water. Small crocodilians are also preyed upon by their larger relatives.

Crocodilians have varied diets and will eat any animal they can catch.

◀ SWALLOWING PREY

A crocodile raises its head and grips a crab firmly at the back of its throat. After several jerky head movements the crab is correctly positioned to be eaten whole. High levels of acid in the crocodile's stomach help it break down the crab's hard shell so that every part is digested.

Did you know? A Nile crocodile has a stomach that is about the size of a basketball.

▶ FISHY FOOD

A Nile crocodile swallows a fish head first. This stops any spines it has from sticking in the crocodile's throat. About 70 percent of the diet of most crocodilians is fish. Crocodilians with narrow snouts, such as the gharial, Johnston's crocodile and the African slender-snouted crocodile, feed mainly on fish. Fish are caught with a sideways, snapping movement that is easier and faster with a slender snout.

Focus on a

1 A Nile crocodile is nearly invisible, as it lies almost submerged in wait for its prey. Only its eyes, ears and nostrils are showing. It lurks in places where it knows prey regularly visit the river. Its dark olive color provides effective camouflage. To disappear completely it can vanish beneath the water. Some crocodilians can hold their breath for more than an hour while submerged.

A crocodile quietly drifting near the shore looks just like a harmless, floating log. This is just a disguise as it waits for an unsuspecting animal to come down to the river to drink. The crocodile is in luck. A herd of zebras come to cross the river. The crocodile launches its attack with astonishing speed. Shooting forward, it snaps shut its powerful jaws and sharp teeth like a vice around a zebra's leg or muzzle. The stunned zebra is pulled into deeper water to be drowned. Other crocodiles are attracted to the large kill. They gather around to bite into the carcass, rotating in the water to twist off large chunks of flesh. Grazing animals constantly risk death-by-crocodile to drink or cross water. There is little they can do to defend themselves from the attack of such a large predator.

2 The crocodile erupts from the water, taking the zebras by surprise. It lunges at its victim with a quick burst of energy. It is important for the crocodile to overcome its prey quickly, as it cannot chase it overland. The crocodile is also easily exhausted and takes a long time to recover from exercise of any kind.

Crocodile's Lunch

3 The crocodile seizes, pulls and shakes the zebra in its powerful jaws. Sometimes the victim's neck is broken in the attack, and it dies quickly. More often the shocked animal is dragged into the water, struggling feebly against its attacker.

4 The crocodile drags the zebra into deeper water and holds it down to drown it. It may also spin around, until the prey stops breathing. The crocodile continues to spin around with the prey clamped in its jaws, until it is dead.

5 A freshly killed zebra attracts Nile crocodiles from all around. A large kill is too difficult for one crocodile to defend on its own. Several crocodiles take turns sharing the feast and may help each other tear the carcass apart. They fasten their jaws onto a leg or lump of muscle and twist it in the water like a rotating shaft, until a chunk of meat is torn loose and can be swallowed.

Communication

Crocodilians pass on messages to each other by means of sounds, body language, smells and touch. Unlike other reptiles, they have a remarkable social life. Groups gather together for basking, sharing food, courting and nesting. Communication begins in the egg and continues throughout life. Adults are particularly sensitive to hatchling and juvenile distress calls and respond with threats or actual attacks. Sounds are made with the vocal cords and with other parts of the body, such as slapping the head against the surface of the water. Crocodilians also use visual communication. Body postures and special movements show which individuals are strong and dominant. Weaker individuals signal to show that they recognize a dominant individual to avoid fighting and injury.

▲ **HEAD BANGER**
A crocodile lifts its head out of the water, jaws open. The jaws slam shut just before they smack the surface of the water. This is called the head slap and makes a loud pop followed by a splash. Head slapping may be a sign of dominance and is often used during the breeding season.

The Fox and the Crocodile
In this Aesop's fable, the fox and the crocodile meet one day. The crocodile boasts at length about its cunning as a hunter. Then the fox says, "That's all very impressive, but tell me, what am I wearing on my feet?" The crocodile looks down and there, on the fox's feet, is a pair of shoes made from crocodile skin.

▲ **GHARIAL MESSAGES**
The gharial does not head slap, but claps its jaws underwater during the breeding season. Sound travels faster through water than air, so sound signals are very useful for aquatic life.

▶ INFRASOUNDS

Some crocodilians make sounds by rapidly squeezing their torso muscles just beneath the surface of the water. The water bubbles up and bounces off the back. The sounds produced are at a very low level, so we can hardly hear them. At close range, they sound like distant thunder. These infrasounds travel quickly over long distances through the water and may be part of courtship. Sometimes they are produced before bellowing, roaring or head slaps.

Did you know? The bellow of an alligator can be heard at least 490 ft away.

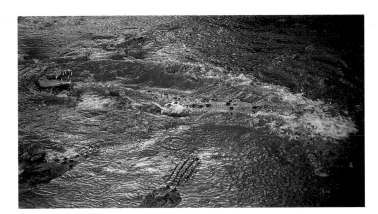

◀ I AM THE GREATEST

Dominant animals are usually bigger and more aggressive than submissive ones. They show off their importance by swimming boldly at the surface or thrashing their tails from side to side on land. Weaker individuals usually only lift their heads out of the water and expose their vulnerable throats. This shows that they submit and do not want to fight.

▶ GETTING TOGETHER

These caimans are gathering together at the start of the rainy season in Brazil. Crocodilians often come together in loose groups—for example, when they are basking, nesting or sharing food. They tend to ignore each other once dominance battles have been established. During a long, dry spell, large numbers of crocodilians often gather together at water holes to share the remaining water. Young crocodilians stay in a close group for the first months of life as there is safety in numbers.

Choosing a Mate

Male and female crocodilians are often difficult to tell apart. Only male gharials are immediately recognizable, distinguished from females by the bumps on the ends of their snouts. Most males are larger, and grow and mature more quickly than females. They are ready to mate at about seven years old; females are ready at about nine.

In some species, groups of adults gather in the breeding season and set up special mating territories. In other species, mating takes place in long-established territories. Females often begin the courtship process. Courtship behavior includes bellowing and grunting, rubbing heads and bodies, blowing bubbles, circling and riding on the partner's back.

▲ BUMPY NOSE
Most male gharials have a strange bump, or pot, on the end of the snout near their nostrils. Females have flat snouts. No one is quite sure what the bump is for, but it is probably used in courtship. It may help the male to change hissing sounds into buzzing sounds, as air vibrates inside the hollow bump.

◄ COURTING COUPLE
Crocodilians touch each other a lot during courtship, especially around the head and neck. Males will also try to impress females by bubbling water from the nostrils and mouth. An interested female arches her back, then raises her head with her mouth open. The two may push each other underwater to see how big and strong their partner is.

◄ SWEET-SMELLING SCENT

Crocodilians have little bumps under their lower jaws. These are musk glands. The musk is a sweet-smelling, greenish, oily perfume. It produces a scent that attracts the opposite sex. Musk glands are more noticeable in males. During courtship, the male may rub his throat across the female's head and neck. This releases the scent from the musk glands and helps to prepare the female for mating.

► FIGHTING MALES

Male crocodilians may fight each other for the chance to court and mate with females. They may spar with their jaws open or make themselves look bigger and more powerful by puffing up their bodies with air. Saltwater crocodiles are particularly violent and bash their heads together with a loud thud. These contests may go on for an hour or more but do not seem to cause much permanent damage.

◄ THE MATING GAME

Courtship can last for up to two hours before mating occurs. The couple sinks underwater, and the male wraps his tail around his partner. Mating takes only a few minutes. The couple mates several times during the day. A dominant male may mate with up to 20 females in the breeding season. Females, too, mate with other males, although the dominant male tries to prevent this.

29

Focus on

Early in April or May, American alligators begin courtship rituals. Males fight each other to win their own territories. The biggest and strongest males win the best territories. Their musk glands give off a strong, sweet smell, attractive to females. Female alligators do not have territories. They visit the territories of several males and may mate several times. Once a female and a male have mated, they part. The female builds a nest in June or July and lays her eggs. In about 60 to 70 days, the young alligators begin to hatch and the female digs them out of the nest and carries them to water. She remains with her young for months or even years.

1 Male and female alligators do not live together all year round. They come together in spring to court and mate. The rest of the year they glide through the swamp, searching for food or basking in the sun. In winter they rest in cozy dens.

2 The American alligator is the noisiest crocodilian. Males and females make bellowing noises especially in the breeding season. Males bellow loudly to warn other males to keep out of their territories and to let females know where they are. Each alligator has a different voice, which sounds like the throaty roar of a stalling motorboat engine. The sound carries for long distances in the swamp. Once one alligator starts to bellow, others soon join in and may continue for half an hour.

Alligators

3 In the mating season bulls (males) test each other to see who is the biggest and strongest. They push and wrestle and sometimes fight violently. The strongest males win the best territories for food and water. Bellowing helps to limit serious fighting. Other males stay away from areas where they have heard a loud bull.

4 Alligators mate in shallow water. Before mating, there is a slow courtship consisting of slapping the water and rubbing each other's muzzle and neck. Mating usually lasts only a minute or two before the pair separates. Alligators may mate with several partners in a season.

5 The female alligator uses her body, legs and tail to build a nest out of sand, soil and plants. It takes about two weeks to build and may be up to 30 in. high and 6 ft across. In the middle the female digs a hole and lines it with mud. She lays between 20 and 70 eggs, which she then covers up. She stays near the nest site while the eggs develop, guarding them from raccoons and other predators.

Building a Nest

About a month after mating, a female crocodilian is ready to lay her eggs on land. First she builds a nest to keep her eggs warm. If the temperature stays below 82°F, the babies will die before they hatch. The temperature inside the nest determines whether the hatchlings are male or female. Females build their nests at night. Alligators, caimans and some crocodiles build nests that are solid mounds of fresh plants and soil. Other crocodiles, and gharials, dig holes in the sand with their back feet. Some species dig trial nests before they dig the real one. This may be to check that the temperature is right for the eggs to develop. Nest sites are chosen to be near water but above the floodwater mark. The females often stay close to the nest to guard it against predators, even while searching for food.

▲ **SHARING NESTS**
Turtles, such as this red-bellied turtle, sometimes lay their eggs in crocodilian nests to save them the hard work of making their own nests. The eggs are protected by the fierce crocodilian mother, who guards her own eggs and the turtle's eggs. As many as 200 red-bellied turtle eggs have been found in alligator nests.

◄ **NEST MOUNDS**
A Morelet's crocodile has raked soil and uprooted plant material into a big pile to build her nest mound. She uses her body to press it all together firmly. Then she scoops out a hole in the mound with her back feet. She lays her eggs in the hole and then closes the top of the nest. As the plant material rots, it gives off heat, which keeps the eggs warm.

Did you know? Male crocodilians do not help make nests.

32

▼ IS IT A BOY OR A GIRL?

A saltwater crocodile, like all crocodilians, keeps its eggs at about 86 to 89°F inside the nest. The temperatures during the first few weeks after the eggs are laid is crucial. This controls whether the babies are male or female. Higher temperatures, such as 89 to 91°F produce more males, while temperatures of 88°F or lower produce more females. Temperature also affects the color and body patterns of the babies.

▲ A SANDY NEST

Nile crocodiles dig their nests on sandy river banks, beaches or lakesides. Females may compete for nest sites by trying to push each other over. Larger, heavier females usually win these contests. The female uses her back legs for digging, so the nest burrow is dug to a depth of about the same length as her back legs.

► NESTING TOGETHER

Female Nile crocodiles often nest together. A female may even return to the same breeding ground and nest site each year. Each female guards her nest, either by lying right on top of the nest or watching it from the nearby shade.

◄ NEST THIEF

The monitor lizard often digs its way into crocodile nests in Africa and Asia to eat the eggs. In Africa, these lizards may sometimes steal over half of all the eggs laid.

Developing Eggs

All crocodilians lay white, oval eggs with hard shells like those of a bird. The number of eggs laid by one female at a time varies from about 10 to 90, depending on the species and the age of the mother. Older females lay more eggs. The length of time it takes for the eggs to hatch varies with the species and the temperature, but takes from 55 to 110 days. During this time, called the incubation period, the weather can affect the babies developing inside the eggs. Too much rain can drown the babies before they are born as water can seep through the shells. Hot weather may cause the inside of the egg to overheat. This hardens the yolk so that the baby cannot absorb it and starves to death. Another danger is that eggs laid by one female are accidentally dug up and destroyed by another female digging a nest in the same place.

▲ **HANDFUL OF EGGS**
In many countries, people eat crocodilian eggs. They harvest them from nests for sale at the local market. This person is holding the eggs of a gharial. Each egg weighs about 3 oz. The mother gharial lays about 40 eggs in a hole in the sand. She lays them in two tiers, separated from each other by a fairly thick layer of sand, and may spend several hours covering her nest.

▶ **LAYING EGGS**
The mugger, or swamp, crocodile of India digs a sandy pit about 20 in. deep in a river bank and lays 10 to 50 eggs inside. She lays her eggs in layers and then covers them with a mound of twigs, leaves, soil and sand. During the 50- to 75-day incubation, the female spends most of the time practically on top of the nest. When females lay their eggs, they are usually quite tame. Researchers have been able to catch the eggs as they are laid.

▶ INSIDE AN EGG

Curled tightly inside its egg, this alligator has its head and tail twisted around its belly. Next to the developing baby is a supply of yolk, which provides it with food during incubation. Researchers have removed the top third of the shell to study the stages of development. The baby will develop normally even though some of the shell is missing. As the eggs develop, they give off carbon dioxide gas into the nest. This reacts with air in the chamber and may make the shell thinner to let in more oxygen.

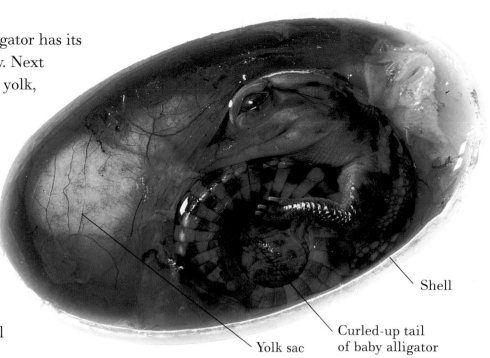

Shell

Curled-up tail of baby alligator

Yolk sac

◀ CRACKING EGGS

Mother crocodiles sometimes help eggs to hatch. When she hears the baby calling inside, she picks up the egg in her mouth. Holding it gently, she rolls the egg back and forth against the roof of her mouth, pressing gently to crack the shell. The mother may have to do this for about 20 minutes before the baby breaks free from the egg.

Did you know? A large crocodile may take an hour to lay 80 or more eggs.

▶ EGGS IN THE NEST

Saltwater crocodiles lay large, creamy-white eggs, up to twice the size of chickens' eggs. However, the eggs are more equally rounded at each end than chicken's eggs. It takes a female saltwater crocodile about 15 minutes to lay between 20 and 90 eggs in her nest. The eggs take up to 90 days to hatch.

Focus on

Baby crocodilians make yelping, croaking and grunting noises from inside their eggs when it is time to hatch. The mother hears the noises and digs the eggs from the nest. The babies struggle free of their eggshells, sometimes with help from their mother. While the young are hatching, the mother is in a very aggressive mood and will attack any animal that comes near. The hatchlings are about 11 inches long, lively and very agile. They can give a human finger a painful nip with their sharp teeth. Their mother carries them gently in her mouth down to the water. She opens her jaws and gently twists her head from side to side to wash the babies out of her mouth.

1 As soon as a mother Nile crocodile hears her babies calling from inside their eggs, she knows it is time to help them escape from the nest. She scrapes off the soil and sand with her front feet and may even use her teeth to cut through any roots that have grown between the eggs. Her help is very important, as the soil has hardened during incubation. The hatchlings would find it difficult to dig their way up to the surface without her help.

The hatchling punches a hole in its hard shell with a forward-pointing egg tooth.

2 This baby Nile crocodile has just broken through its eggshell. It used a horny tip on the snout, called the egg tooth to break through. The egg tooth is the size of a grain of sand and disappears after about a week. The egg has become thinner during the long incubation. This makes it easier for the baby to break free.

Hatching

3 Struggling out of an egg is a long, exhausting process for the hatchling. When the babies are half out of their eggs, they sometimes take a break so they can rest before completely leaving their shells. After hatching, the mother crushes or swallows rotten eggs.

4 Even though they are fierce predators, crocodilians make caring parents. The mother Nile crocodile lowers her head into the nest and delicately picks up the hatchlings, as well as any unhatched eggs, between her sharp teeth. She puts them into her mouth. The weight of all the babies and eggs pushes down on her tongue to form a pouch that holds up to 20 eggs and live young. Male mugger crocodiles also carry the young like this and help hatchlings to escape from their eggs.

5 A young crocodilian's belly looks fat when it hatches. This is because it contains the remains of the yolk sac, which nourished it through the incubation period. The hatchling can swim and catch its own food right away, but it continues to feed on the yolk sac for up to two weeks. In Africa, the wet season usually starts soon after baby Nile crocodiles hatch. This provides an abundance of food, such as insects, tadpoles, and frogs for the hatchlings. They are very vulnerable to predators and are guarded by their mother for a least the first weeks of life.

Growing Up

Juvenile (young) crocodilians lead a very dangerous life. They are too small to defend themselves easily, despite their sharp teeth. Their bright colors also make them easy for predators to spot. All sorts of predators lurk in the water and on the shore, from birds of prey and monitor lizards to otters, pelicans, tiger fish and even other crocodilians. One of the reasons that crocodilians lay so many eggs is that so many young do not survive to reach their first birthday. Only one in ten alligators lives to the end of its first year. Juveniles often stay together in groups during the first weeks of life and call loudly to the adults for help if they are in danger. By the time the juveniles are four years old, they stop making distress calls and start responding to the calls of other young individuals.

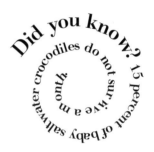

▲ INSECT DIET

A spiky-jawed Johnston's crocodile is about to snap up a damselfly. Juveniles eat mainly insects. As they grow, they take larger prey, such as snails, shrimps, crabs and small fish. Their snouts gradually strengthen, so that they are able to catch bigger prey. At a few months old, they live much like lizards and move quite a distance away from the water.

Did you know? 15 percent of baby saltwater crocodiles do not survive a month.

◄ FAST FOOD

These juvenile alligators will grow twice as fast in captivity as they would in the wild. This is because they are fed regular meals and do not have to wait until they can catch a meal for themselves. It is also because they are kept in warm water—alligators stop feeding in cooler water. The best temperature for growth is 86 to 90°F.

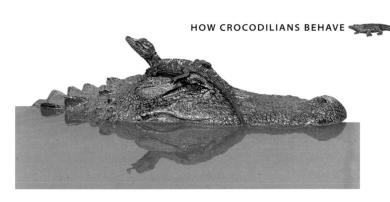

▶ BABY CARRIERS

Juveniles stay close to their mother for the first few weeks, often using her back to rest on. No predator would dare to attack them there. Baby alligators are only about 10 in. long when they are born but they grow very quickly. When they have enough food to eat, male alligators grow about 12 in. a year until they are 15 years of age.

▲ CROC AND POD

A Nile crocodile guards her young while they bask in the sun. A group of crocodilian young is called a pod. A pod may stay in the same area for as long as two years. At the first sign of danger, the mother rapidly vibrates her trunk muscles, and the young immediately dive underwater.

▲ TOO MANY ENEMIES

The list of land predators that attack juvenile crocodilians include big cats such as this leopard, ground hornbills, marabou storks and genet cats. Large wading birds, including herons, spear them with their sharp beaks in shallow water while, in deeper water, catfish, otters and turtles all enjoy a young crocodilian as a snack. Only about two percent of all the eggs laid each year survive to hatch and grow into adults.

▶ NOISY POD

A pod of juveniles, like this group of young caimans, is a noisy bunch. By chirping and yelping for help, a juvenile warns its brothers and sisters that there is a predator nearby. The siblings quickly dive for shelter and hope that an adult will come to protect them. If a young Nile crocodile strays from its pod, it makes loud distress calls. Its mother, or any other female nearby, will pick up the youngster in her jaws and carry it back to the group.

On the Defensive

By the time a crocodilian has grown to about 3 feet long, very few predators will threaten it. The main dangers to adult crocodilians come from large animals, such as jaguars, lions, elephants and hippopotamuses, who attack to protect their young. Giant snakes called anacondas will attack and kill crocodilians for food. Adults may also be killed during battles with other crocodilians during the breeding season. People are the main enemy of crocodilians. They kill them for their skins, for food or when they become dangerous. Crocodilians are protected by their powerful jaws, strong tail and heavy armor. They can also swim away from danger and hide underwater, in the mud or among plants.

▲ **KEEP AWAY!**
An American alligator puffs up its body with air to look bigger and more threatening. It lets out the air quickly to make a hissing sound. If an enemy is still not scared away, the alligator will then attack.

► **THE HIDDEN EYE**
What sort of animal is peeping out from underneath a green carpet of floating water plants? It is hard to tell that there is a saltwater crocodile lurking just beneath the surface. Crocodilians feel safer in the water because they are such good swimmers. They may spend hours almost completely underwater, keeping very still, waiting for prey to come by or for danger to pass. They move so quietly and smoothly that the vegetation on top of the water is hardly disturbed.

▶ CAMOUFLAGE COLORS

The color of crocodilians blends in well with their surroundings. Many species change color all the time. For example, at warmer times of the day, they may become lighter in color. During cool parts of the day, such as the morning, they may look duller and are often mistaken for logs.

◀ CAIMAN FOR LUNCH

A deadly anaconda squeezes the life out of an unfortunate caiman. The anaconda of South America lives partly in the water and can grow up to 30 ft long. It can easily kill a caiman by twisting its strong coils around the caiman's body until the victim cannot breathe any more. The caiman dies slowly, either from suffocation or shock. However, anacondas only kill caimans occasionally—they are not an important part of the snake's diet.

Ticking Croc
One of the most famous crocodiles in literature is in Peter Pan, *written by J. M. Barrie in 1904. Peter Pan's greatest enemy is Captain Hook. In a fair fight, Peter cuts off Hook's left hand, which is eaten by a crocodile. The crocodile follows Hook's ship, hoping for a chance to gobble up the rest of him. He makes a ticking noise as he travels because he swallowed a clock. At the end, Hook falls into the water. He is chased by the crocodile, but we do not find out if he eats him.*

▲ HUMAN DANGERS

People have always killed small numbers of crocodilians for food, as this Brazilian family has done. However, the shooting of crocodilians through fear or for sport has had a much more severe impact on their population. Of the 22 species of crocodilian, 17 have been hunted to the verge of extinction.

Freshwater Habitats

A habitat is a place where an animal lives. Most crocodilians live in freshwater habitats, such as rivers, lakes, marshes and swamps, and in warm places. They tend to live in shallow areas because they need to be able to crawl onto dry land for basking and laying their eggs. The shallow water also has many plants to hide among and plenty of animals to eat. The temperature of the water does not vary as much as temperatures on dry land do. This helps a crocodilian keep its body temperature steady. Crocodilians save energy by moving around in water rather than on dry land because the water supports their heavy bodies. Crocodilians also make an impact on their habitats. The American alligator, for example, digs holes in the river bed. These are cool places where alligators and other animals hide during the heat of the day.

▲ **GATOR HOLES**
American alligators living in the Florida Everglades dig large gator holes in the limestone river bed. In the dry season, these holes stay full of water. They provide a vital water supply that keeps the alligators and many other animals alive.

▲ **RIVER DWELLERS**
The gharial likes fast-flowing rivers with high banks, clear water and deep pools where there are plenty of fish. It inhabits rivers such as the Indus in Pakistan, the Ganges in India and the Brahmaputra of Bangladesh and Assam.

Aboriginal Creation Myth
Crocodiles are often shown in bark paintings and rock art made by the Aboriginals of Australia. Their creation myth, called the "dream time," tells how ancestral animals created the land and people. According to a  *Gunwinggu story from Arnhem Land, the Liverpool River was made by a crocodile ancestor. The mighty crocodile made his way from the mountains to the sea, chewing the land as he went. This made deep furrows, which filled with water to become the river.*

◄ SEASONAL CHANGE

During the dry season, caimans gather in the few remaining pools along a drying-up river bed. Although the pools become very crowded, the caimans seem to get along well together. In some parts of South America, caimans are forced to live in river pools for four or five months of the year. After the floods of the wet season, they can spread out again.

► NILE CROCODILES

Nile crocodiles warm themselves in the sun on a sandy riverbank. Despite their name, Nile crocodiles do not live only in the river Nile. At one time, these powerful crocodiles lived all over Africa, except in the desert areas. Nowadays, they still live in parts of the Nile, as well as the other African waterways such as the Limpopo and Senegal rivers, Lake Chad and the Okavango swamp. There are also Nile crocodiles living on the island of Madagascar.

◄ AUSTRALIAN HABITATS

Australian crocodiles, such as Johnston's crocodile, often live in billabongs (waterholes), such as this one in the Northern Territory of Australia. They provide crocodiles with water and land as well as food to eat. A billabong is a branch of a river that comes to a dead end. Saltwater crocodiles are also found in such areas because they live in both fresh and salt water. People are advised not to swim or wade in the water and to avoid camping nearby.

Rainforest Dwellers

Three unusual crocodilians live in rainforest streams and swamps where they avoid competition with larger caimans and crocodiles. Cuvier's dwarf caiman and Schneider's dwarf caiman live in South America, while the African dwarf crocodile lives in the tropical forests of Central Africa. The bodies of these small crocodilians are heavily armored. This may help to protect the South American caimans from sharp rocks in the fast-flowing streams where they live and from spiky plants in the forest. All three crocodilians may also need this extra protection from predators because of their small size. Rainforest crocodilians do not usually bask in the sun during the day, although the dwarf crocodile may sometimes climb trees to sun itself. All three crocodilians seem to spend quite a lot of time on land. Schneider's dwarf caiman lives in burrows dug in stream banks.

▲ MYSTERIOUS CROC

Very little is known about the African dwarf crocodile. It is a secretive and shy animal that is active at night. It lives in swamps, ponds and small, slow-moving streams. After heavy rain, the dwarf crocodile may make long trips over land at night. Females lay about ten eggs, which take 100 days to hatch. They probably protect their young in their first weeks.

Did you know? Cuvier's dwarf caimans sometimes eat their own young.

◄ YOUNG COLORS

A newly hatched Cuvier's dwarf caiman rests on a rock. Hatchling dwarf caimans have a yellowish-brown skull and black or brown crossbands on the body and tail. This is helpful for camouflage. For the first couple of days, they are also covered in slime. Then they enter the water for the first time.

Termite mound

Schneider's dwarf
Caiman eggs

Caiman nest

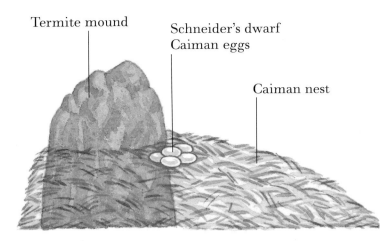

Termite
mound

Edge of nest

82°F

83°F

84°F

86°F

90°F

93°F

3 feet

◄ HELPFUL NEIGHBORS

Schneider's dwarf caiman lays its eggs beside
termite mounds. Little sun reaches the forest
floor, so the extra heat generated by the termites
helps the caiman's eggs develop. Often, the
termites cover the eggs with a rock-hard layer, so
the parents must help their young break out.

▲ NOSE TO TAIL

Unlike other caimans, dwarf caimans do not
have bony ridges around the eyes and snout.
Because of this they are also known as smooth-
fronted caimans. Shown here is Cuvier's dwarf
caiman. Its short snout is not streamlined for
swimming, and it has a short tail, which may
help it to move more easily on land.

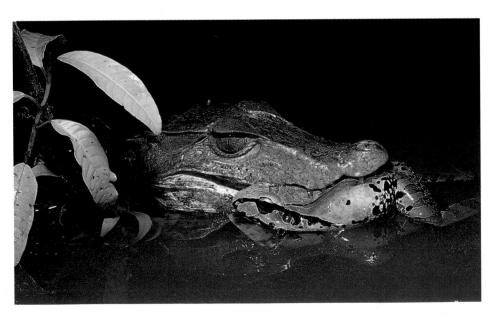

◄ TEETH AND DIET

The sharp, pointed teeth of
Cuvier's dwarf caiman curve
backward in the mouth. This
helps it grip the slippery skin of
frogs or seize such prey as fish
in fast-flowing waters. The
Cuvier's diet is not well known,
but it probably eats a variety of
aquatic invertebrates (animals
without a backbone), such as
shrimps and crabs, as well as
rodents, birds and snakes.

MARKINGS FOR LIFE

A black caiman hatches from its egg. Its mother laid up to 65 eggs in the nest, which hatched six weeks later. Its strong markings stay as it grows.

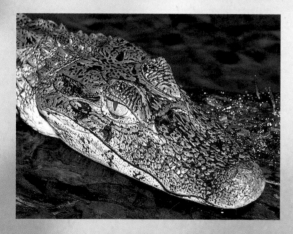

THE SPECTACLED CAIMAN

The spectacled caiman is so-called because of the bony ridges around its eye sockets and across the top of the muzzle. These look a bit like eye glasses and may help to strengthen its skull as it seizes and kills prey.

BIG HEAD

The broad-snouted caiman has the widest head of any crocodilian, with a ridge running down the snout. It is about 6 ft long and lives in marshes or small streams with dense vegetation.

Focus on

Caimans are mostly small, agile crocodilians that live in Central or South America. Most do not grow more than 7 feet long, but the black caiman can be bigger than an alligator (their closest relative). Caimans look like alligators because their lower teeth do not show when their mouths are closed. They have sharper, longer teeth than alligators and strong, bony plates on the belly and back, including eight bony scutes on the back of the neck. This bony armor helps to protect them from predators, even humans (as tough skin is unsuitable for leather goods). Many caimans are endangered, but some spectacled caimans are very adaptable. They have taken over habitats where American crocodiles and black caimans have been hunted to extinction.

Caimans

Young caimans have spots and bands across the body.

Black caiman
(Melanosuchus niger)

Bony scutes

Unusual webbed front feet

Short, low snout with jaws lined with 64 teeth

MEMBERS OF THE GATOR CLAN

Caimans have short snouts, roughly circular eye sockets and wrinkled eyelids. Although caimans are closely related to alligators, they are quicker and move more like crocodiles.

EGG THIEF

Tegu lizards eat caiman eggs. In some areas, over 80 percent of the nests are destroyed by these large lizards. Female caimans may nest together to help defend their eggs.

CAPABLE CAIMAN

The black caiman is the largest of all caimans. The one shown here has just snapped up a piranha. Black caimans can grow to over 19 ft long and have sharp eyesight and hearing. They hunt for capybaras (South American rodents) and fish after dusk. When black caimans disappear, the balance of life in an area is upset. Hunted for killing cattle, they are now an endangered species.

Saltwater Species

Most crocodilians live in fresh water, but a few venture into estuaries (the mouths of rivers), coastal swamps or the sea. American and Nile crocodiles and spectacled caimans have been found in saltwater habitats. The crocodilian most often seen at sea is the saltwater crocodile, also known as the Indopacific or estuarine crocodile. It is found in a vast area, from southern India to Fiji, and although usually found in rivers and lakes, it has been seen hundreds of miles from the nearest land. Hatchlings are even reared in seawater. This species has efficient salt glands on its tongue to get rid of extra salt without losing too much water. It is a mystery why freshwater crocodiles also have these glands, but it may be because their ancestors lived in the sea. Alligators and caimans do not have salt glands.

▲ **SALTY TONGUE**
Crocodiles have up to 40 salt glands on the tongue. These special salivary glands let the crocodile get rid of excess salt without losing too much water. These glands are necessary because crocodiles have kidneys that need plenty of water to flush out the salt. At sea there is too little fresh water for this to happen.

► **SCALY DRIFTER**
Although it can swim vast distances far out to sea, a saltwater crocodile is generally a lazy creature. Slow, side-to-side sweeps of a long, muscular tail propel the crocodile through the water, using as little energy as possible. Saltwater crocodiles do not like to have to swim vigorously, so they avoid strong waves wherever possible. They prefer to drift with the tide in relatively calm water.

► **NEW WORLD CROC**

The American crocodile is the most widespread crocodile in the Americas, ranging from southern Florida to the Pacific coat of Peru. It grows up to 19 ft in length (11 ft on average) and lives in mangrove swamps, estuaries and lagoons as well as fresh and brackish (slightly salty) coastal rivers.

It has the least armor (bony scutes) of any crocodilian and a hump on the snout between the eyes and nostrils.

◄ **TRAVELING CAIMANS**

A group of baby spectacled, or common, caimans hides among the leaves of aquatic plants. This wide-ranging species lives in all sorts of habitats, including saltwater ones, such as salt marshes. They even live on islands, such as Trinidad and Tobago in the Caribbean.

◄ **LOST ARMOR**

A saltwater crocodile has less protective armor on the neck and back compared to other crocodilians. This makes it easier for the crocodile to bend its body when swimming. Thick, heavy scales would weigh it down too much at sea.

▲ **NILE CROCODILE**

Nile crocodiles typically live in rivers, but they also inhabit salty estuaries and mangrove swamps. Sometimes they are found on Kenyan beaches and may be swept out to sea. Some have reached the islands of Zanzibar and Madagascar.

49

Ancient Crocodiles

The first alligators and crocodiles lived at the same time as the dinosaurs. Some were even powerful enough to kill the biggest plant-eating dinosaurs. Unlike the dinosaurs, the crocodilians have managed to survive to the present day, possibly because they were so well adapted to their environment. The first crocodiles, the protosuchians, lived about 200 million years ago. They were small land animals with long legs and short snouts. From 200 to 65 million years ago, long-snouted mesosuchians lived mainly in the sea, while the dinosaurs dominated the land. The closest ancestors of today's crocodilians were the early eusuchians, which developed about 80 million years ago. They looked much like gharials, with long snouts, and probably lurked in the shallow fresh waters of rivers and swamps. Like today's crocodilians, the eusuchians could breathe through their nostrils even when their mouths were open underwater. This made it possible for them to catch their prey in the water.

▲ **FIRST CROCODILE**
The name of this ancient crocodile, *Protosuchus*, means "first crocodile." It lived about 200 million years ago in Arizona and looked much like a lizard. *Protosuchus* was small, probably no more than 3 ft long, with a small, flat skull and a short snout.

▼ **BACK TO THE SEA**
Swimming along the shores and estuaries in Jurassic times, from about 200 to 145 million years ago, the most widespread crocodilian was *Stenosaurus*. It looked like modern-day gharials, although it is not related to them. *Stenosaurus* had a flexible body and a powerful tail, which allowed it to swim after fast-moving prey.

Long, slender snout and up to 200 piercing teeth for trapping fish

50

► **DINOSAUR DAYS**

Goniopholis, shown here, was more dependent on land than many of its fellow mesosuchians. It looked much like a broad-snouted crocodile of today. *Goniopholis* had two or more rows of armor on its back and well-developed armor on its belly as well. Most mesosuchians lived in the sea. They were long-snouted with many piercing teeth for catching fish.

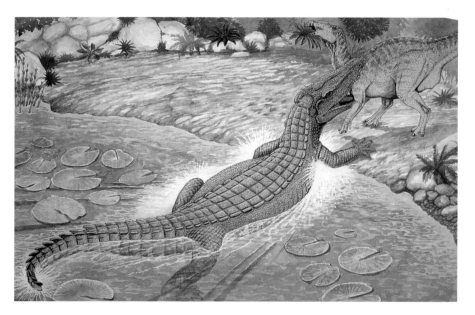

◄ **MONSTER CROCODILE**

Lurking in rivers and lakes 70 million years ago was a gigantic crocodile called *Deinosuchus,* which grew perhaps 50 ft long. It was a similar size to *T. rex* and big enough to eat quite large dinosaurs, such as the duck-billed dinosaurs. It had strong teeth and legs, vertebrae (spine bones) that were each 12 in. long and heavy protective scales shielding the body and the tail.

► **SURVIVORS**

Crocodilians are survivors of a world inhabited by dinosaurs. However, the origins of both dinosaurs and crocodilians date back much further, to a group of animals called thecodontians, which lived some 200 million years ago.

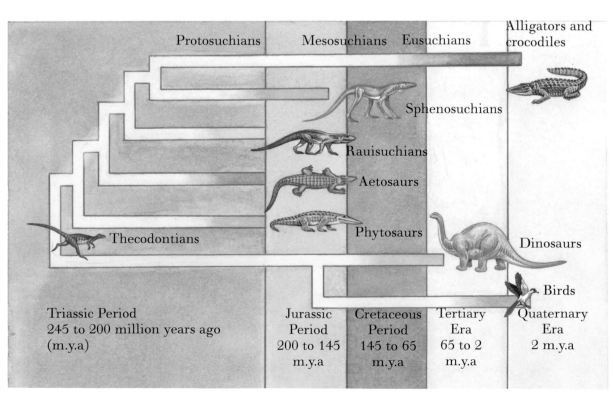

Protosuchians   Mesosuchians   Eusuchians

Alligators and crocodiles

Sphenosuchians

Rauisuchians

Aetosaurs

Thecodontians

Phytosaurs

Dinosaurs

Birds

Triassic Period
245 to 200 million years ago
(m.y.a)

Jurassic
Period
200 to 145
m.y.a

Cretaceous
Period
145 to 65
m.y.a

Tertiary
Era
65 to 2
m.y.a

Quaternary
Era
2 m.y.a

51

Living Relatives

Although it seems strange, birds are probably the closest living relatives of crocodilians. Crocodilians and birds have a long outer ear canal, a muscular gizzard to grind up food and a heart made up of four chambers. They both build nests and look after their young. The next closest living relatives of crocodilians are the group of reptiles called lepidosaurs, which includes the tuatara of New Zealand, lizards and snakes. The skin of lepidosaurs is usually covered by overlapping scales made of keratin (the substance fingernails are made of). Crocodilians and lepidosaurs both have two large openings on the cheek region of the skull, called a diapsid skull. Crocodilians are also more distantly related to the other main group of reptiles, turtles and tortoises.

▼ DINOSAUR SURVIVOR

The rare tuatara is found only on a few islands off the north coast of New Zealand. Here there are no rats or dogs to eat their eggs and hatchlings. They have hardly changed in appearance for millions of years and first appeared before dinosaurs lived on the earth.

▲ NESTING HABITS

The nests of some birds, such as this mallee fowl, are very similar to those of crocodilians. The mallee fowl builds a huge mound of wet leaves and twigs covered with wet sand. The female then lays her eggs in the middle of the mound.

▲ A SANDY NEST

Green turtles live in the sea, but lay their eggs on sandy beaches. The female drags herself up the beach and digs a hole in which to lay her eggs. Then she returns to the sea, leaving the baby turtles to fend for themselves when they eventually hatch.

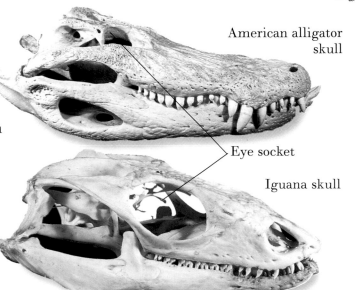

American alligator skull

Eye socket

Iguana skull

► DIAPSID SKULLS

Crocodilians, and lizards such as iguanas, both have two large openings on each side of the skull behind the eye sockets. One of these windows is high on the roof of the skull, the other is down on the side of the cheek. These openings may be to make the skull lighter. They also provide areas for the jaw muscles to attach on to the skull, making it stronger and more powerful. In birds, the two openings have largely disappeared. Mammals have only one opening on each side, not two, while turtles have no openings at all.

Red-tailed boa

▲ REPTILE PREDATOR

Snakes are also scaly, meat-eating reptiles, but they catch prey in very different ways from a crocodilian. They have delicate bodies and need to overpower prey quickly before it can inflict an injury. Some, such as this boa, squeeze their prey to death in their powerful coils. Others kill their prey with a poisonous bite.

Did you know? The sex of baby turtles is also controlled by temperature.

► MONSTROUS LIZARD

The gila monster of North America is a lizard with small, bead-like scales. It is one of the world's two poisonous lizards, and its bright colors are a warning sign of its poisonous nature. The poison is produced in glands in the bottom jaw and chewed into both predators and prey. Crocodilians have much larger scales than lizards, and none are poisonous.

53

Living with People

Many people only ever see a crocodile or an alligator in a book or magazine, on television or at the cinema. These crocodilians are often huge, fierce monsters that attack and eat humans. Such images have given crocodilians a bad name. A few large crocodile types, such as the Nile and saltwater species, can be very dangerous, but most are timid creatures that are no threat to humans. Some people even keep baby crocodilians as pets. Humans are a much bigger threat to crocodilians than they are to us. People hunt them for their skins to make handbags, shoes and belts. Traditional Asian medicines are made from many of their body parts. Their bones are ground up to add to fertilizers and animal feed. Their meat and eggs are cooked and eaten, while perfume is made from their sex organs, musk and urine.

▲ **ALLIGATOR DANGER**
The barely visible head of an American alligator reinforces why swimming is not allowed. Alligators lurking under the water do occasionally attack people. This usually only happens when humans have invaded their habitat or disturbed nests or hatchlings.

▶ **CROCODILE DUNDEE**
One of the most dangerous and aggressive crocodilians is the saltwater crocodile, which appeared in the film *Crocodile Dundee*. In the film, Mick "Crocodile" Dundee, saves an American journalist from a surprise attack by a saltie. An adult saltie can grow up to 23 ft long and is likely to view a human entering its territory as a possible meal.

Krindlekrax

In Philip Ridley's 1991 story, Krindlekrax, a baby crocodile from a zoo escapes into a sewer and grows enormous on a diet of discarded toast. It becomes the mysterious monster Krindlekrax, which lurks beneath the pavements of Lizard Street. It is eventually tamed by the hero of the book, Ruskin Splinter, who wedges a medal down the crododile's throat. He agrees to take the medal out if Krindlekrax will go back to the sewer and never come back to Lizard Street again.

▲ SKINS FOR SALE

These saltwater crocodile skins are being processed for tanning. Tanning converts the hard, horny, preserved skin into soft, flexible leather that can be made into bags, wallets, shoes and other goods. Some of the most valuable skins come from saltwater crocodiles, because they have small scales that have few bony plates inside.

▲ ALLIGATOR STROLL

An American alligator walks through a campsite, giving the campers a close-up view. Attacks on land are unlikely—the element of surprise is lost, and alligators cannot move fast out of the water. Meetings like this are harmless.

A false, glass eye has been inserted into the head.

▶ TOURIST SOUVENIRS

A baby Siamese crocodile was killed so that its head could be made into a key ring as a tourist souvenir. Most tourists never manage to see a wild crocodilian, but if they buy souvenirs such as this, it means more animals will be killed for a cruel trade.

Rare Crocodilians

Almost half of all of crocodilian species are endangered, even though there is much less hunting today than in the past. Until the 1970s, five to ten million crocodilians were being killed each year—far too many for them to reproduce and build up their numbers again. Today, the loss of habitat is a greater threat than hunting for most crocodiles. Other problems include illegal hunting, trapping for food and medicine and the harvesting of crocodile eggs. Many species are not properly protected in national parks, and there are not enough crocodilians being reared on farms and ranches to make sure each species does not disappear forever. The four most endangered species are the Chinese alligator and the Philippine, Siamese and Orinoco crocodiles. Other species that only live in small populations are the Cuban crocodile, black caiman and the gharial.

▲ **HABITAT DESTRUCTION**
The trees beside this billabong in Australia have died because there is too much salt in the water. Farmers removed many of the bush plants, which used to trap salt and stop it from sinking down into the ground. Now much of the land is ruined by high levels of salt, and it is difficult for crocodilians and other wildlife to live there.

► **FISHING COMPETITION**
People fishing for sport as well as for food create competition for crocodilians in some areas. They may also accidentally trap crocodilians underwater in their fishing nets causing them to drown. In waterways that are used for recreation, such as angling, bathing and boating, crocodilians may be accidentally killed by the blades of a motorboat's engine or intentionally killed because they may pose a threat to human life.

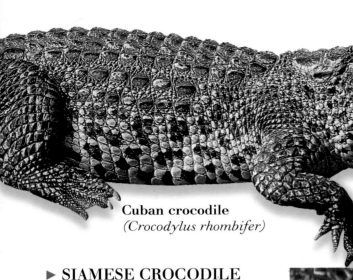

Cuban crocodile
(Crocodylus rhombifer)

◀ CUBAN CROCODILE

This crocodile has the smallest range of any living crocodilian and is seriously endangered. It lives only on the island of Cuba and the nearby Isle of Pines. The growth of charcoal burning has drastically reduced the habitat of the Cuban crocodile. It has also moved into coastal areas and rivers, where it is more in danger from hunters.

▶ SIAMESE CROCODILE

This endangered crocodile has almost died out in the wild. It was once found over large areas of Southeast Asia, but wild Siamese crocodiles now live only in Thailand. They have become so rare because of extensive hunting and habitat destruction. They now survive mainly on crocodile farms.

▲ ILLEGAL HUNTING

This poacher has speared a caiman in the Brazilian rainforest. Hunting crocodilians is banned in many countries, but people still hunt illegally in order to make money. Their hides are so valuable that, even though this caiman's skin contains many bony scutes, the soft parts will bring a good price.

▼ UNWANTED CROCODILE

A small saltwater crocodile that strayed into somebody's garden is captured so it can be returned to the wild. Its jaws are bound together with rope to stop it from biting the ranger. One of the biggest problems for crocodilians is the fact that more and more people want to live in the same places that they do.

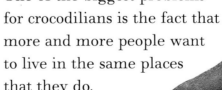

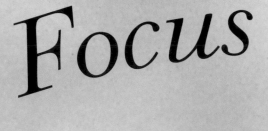

Focus

WELL ADAPTED

Gharials have a light-colored, slender body with extensive webbing between the toes on the back feet. Their long back legs are relatively weak. Gharials are well adapted for life in the water but are not fast swimmers.

The gharial of northern India and the false gharial of Southeast Asia are both endangered species. Their numbers have fallen due to hunting for their skins, habitat loss and competition for their main food, fish. Many of the fast-flowing rivers in which they live have been dammed to provide water for crops and to generate electricity. Dams flood some areas and reduce the flow of water in others, as well as damaging the river banks where gharials nest. People collect their eggs for food and believe them to have medicinal properties. To save the gharial, young are reared in captivity and released into the wild. The false gharial, however, does not breed well in captivity.

CAPTIVE SURVIVAL

This gharial was bred in captivity and has been released into the wild. It has a radio tag on its tail so that scientists can follow its movements. In the 1970s, there were only about 300 wild gharials left. Captive breeding has increased the number to over 1,500.

MEAL TIME

A gharial lunges sideways to snap up a meal from a passing school of fish. Predatory catfish are a favorite meal. When gharial numbers went down, more catfish survived to eat the tilapia fish that local villagers caught for food.

on Gharials

FALSE IDENTITY

The false gharial looks like the true gharial and is probably related to it. It lives farther south than the true gharial, from southern Thailand to Borneo and Sumatra. In the wild, adults do not seem to help their young escape from the nest, and many die as they fend for themselves after hatching. Habitat loss and an increase in land used for rice farming have made false gharials rare. In Indonesia, over-collection of juveniles for rearing on farms may also have reduced numbers.

SAFE HOUSE

A scientist collects gharial eggs so that they can be protected in a sanctuary. There no predators will be able to get at them, and the temperature can be kept just right for development. In the wild, about 40 percent of eggs are destroyed by predators. Only about 1 percent of the young survive to adulthood.

WATER SPORT

In the dry, low-water months of winter, gharials spend a lot of time basking on sand banks. Even so, they are the most aquatic crocodilian. They move awkwardly when leaving the water and do not seem able to do the high walk like other crocodilians. Female gharials do not carry their young to the water. This is probably because their snouts are too slender and delicate and their teeth too sharp.

Conservation

Although people are frightened of crocodilians, they are a vital part of the web of life in tropical lands. They dig water holes that help other animals survive in dry seasons and clean up the environment by eating dead animals. Scientists find them interesting because they are good at fighting disease and rarely develop cancers. They are also fascinating to everyone as survivors from a prehistoric lost world. We need to find out more about their lives in the wild so we can help them to survive in the future. Some species, such as the American alligator, the saltwater crocodile and Johnston's crocodile of Australia and the gharial have already been helped by conservation measures. Much more work needs to be done, however, such as preserving their habitats, stopping illegal poaching and smuggling, breeding rare species in captivity and releasing them into the wild.

▲ CROCODILE FARMS
Tourists watch a wrestler show off his skill at a crocodile farm. The farm breeds crocodiles for their skins, attracting tourists as extra income. Farms help stop crocodiles from being taken from the wild. The Samutprakan Crocodile Farm in Thailand has helped to save the rare Siamese crocodile from dying out by breeding them in captivity.

► RESEARCH REFUGE
Research at the Rockefeller Wildlife Refuge in Louisiana helped determine the best way of rearing American alligators in captivity. They are brought up in special hothouses where temperature, humidity, diet, space and disease can be controlled. They have piped music so they will be less disturbed by outside noises. In these conditions, the alligators grow more than 3 ft a year— much faster than in the wild.

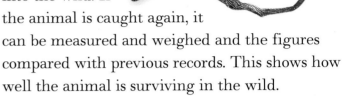

The tag on the foot of a black caiman helps identify it once it has been released into the wild. If the animal is caught again, it can be measured and weighed and the figures compared with previous records. This shows how well the animal is surviving in the wild.

▲ INTO THE FUTURE

This boy from Guyana is holding a baby dwarf caiman. Small numbers of caimans are sold as exotic pets. If people are paid more money for a living specimen than a dead one, they are less likely to kill crocodiles for skins. Educating people about why crocodilians are important is an important way of ensuring their future.

► RANCHING AND FARMING

A Nile crocodile is fed at a breeding station in South Africa. Crocodilians grow well on ranches or farms where they are fed properly. These places also provide information about the biology, health and feeding patterns of the reptiles.

◄ A NEW HOME

A row of black caimans, saved from a ranching development in Bolivia, wait to be flown to the Beni Biosphere Reserve, where they will be protected. The number of black caimans has dropped dramatically, and the animals they used to eat have thrived as a result. This has caused problems for people, such as capybaras eating crops and piranhas attacking cattle.

GLOSSARY

albino
An animal that has no color on all or part of its body but belongs to a species that is usually colored.

bask
To lie for hours in the warmth of the sun, like a person who is sunbathing.

billabong
Branch of a river that comes to a dead end in a backwater or stagnant pool.

camouflage
Colors or patterns on their skins that allow crocodilians to hide in their surroundings.

canine
A sharp, pointed tooth next to the incisors that grips and pierces the skin of prey.

carcass
The dead body of an animal.

cold-blooded
An animal whose body temperature varies with that of its surroundings.

conservation
Protecting living things and helping them to survive in the future.

crocodilian
A member of the group of animals that includes crocodiles, alligators, caimans and gharials.

diaphragm
A sheet of muscle separating the chest cavity from the abdominal cavity, the movement of which helps with breathing.

diapsid
A type of skull with two openings on either side, behind the eye socket.

digestion
The process by which food is broken down so it can be absorbed into the body.

digit
Finger or toe at the end of an animal's limb.

dinosaur
An extinct group of reptiles that lived from 245–65 million years ago.

dominant animal
An animal that the other members of its group allow to take first place.

egg tooth
A small, sharp point on the tip of a baby crocodilian's snout, which helps it to break out of its eggshell.

estuary
The mouth of a large river where it reaches the sea.

gastroliths
Hard objects, such as stones, swallowed by crocodilians, that stay in the stomach to help crush food.

gator
A shortened name for an alligator, commonly used in the United States.

gizzard
A muscular chamber in an animal's gut that grinds large lumps of food into small pieces or particles.

habitat
The place where an animal naturally lives.

incubation
Keeping eggs warm so that development can take place.

infrasounds
Very low sounds which are too low for people to hear.

intestines
Part of an animal's digestive system where food is broken down and absorbed into the body.

invertebrate
An animal that does not have a backbone.

juvenile
A young animal before it grows and develops into a mature adult.

keratin
A horny substance that makes up the scales of lizards, snakes and tuataras.

mammal
An animal with fur or hair and a backbone, that can control its own body temperature. Females feed their young on milk made in mammary glands.

membrane
A thin film, skin or layer.

molar
A chewing and grinding tooth at the side of the jaw.

nictitating membrane
A third eyelid that can be passed over the eye to keep it clean or shield it.

palate
The roof of the mouth. An extra or secondary bony palate separates the mouth from the breathing passages.

poaching
Capturing and/or killing animals illegally and selling them for commercial gain.

pod
A group of young crocodilians just out of their eggs.

predator
An animal that catches and kills other animals for food.

prehistoric
Dating from the time long ago, before people wrote down historical records.

prey
An animal that is hunted and eaten by other animals.

pupil
In animals with backbones, the dark, circular opening in the middle of the eye that allows light to enter.

rainforest
The tropical forest that grows near the equator, where it is hot and wet all year round.

range
The maximum area in which an animal roams.

reptile
A scaly, cold-blooded animal with a backbone, including tortoises, turtles, snakes, lizards and crocodilians.

salivary gland
Gland opening into or near the mouth that produces the fluids in the mouth that start the process of breaking food down for digestion.

scutes
The thick, sometimes bony, scales that cover the bodies of crocodilians.

solar panel
An electric device that turns heat and light from the sun into electric power.

species
A group of animals that share similar characteristics and can breed together to produce fertile young.

swamp
A waterlogged area of land or forest, such as the mangrove swamps that are found in Florida.

territory
An area of land that one or more animals defend against members of the same and other species.

tropics
The hot regions or countries near the equator and between the tropic of Cancer and the tropic of Capricorn.

vocal cords
Two folds of skin in the throats of warm-blooded animals that vibrate and produce sound when air passes through them.

warm-blooded
An animal that can maintain its body at roughly the same warm temperature all the time.

windpipe
In air-breathing animals, the breathing tube that leads from the mouth opening to the lungs.

yolk
Food material rich in protein and fats, which nourishes a developing embryo inside an egg.

INDEX